HAWAII
TRAVEL G

2022

TRAVEL PILOTS

CONTENTS

INTRODUCTION
    WELCOME TO HAWAII
    VARIOUS REASONS TO LOVE HAWAII

HAWAII
    FAMILIARIZING ONESELF WITH
    HONOLULU
    WAIKĪKĪ AND BEYOND
    OʻAHU
    HANAUMA BAY
    MOLOKAʻI AND LĀNAʻI

IMPORTANT DETAILS

A FEW TRAVEL TIPS

INTRODUCTION ▶ WELCOME TO HAWAII

Hawaii is an island paradise with golden sands, palm palms that sway in the wind, lush valleys, and turquoise water teeming with tropical fish. For many individuals, seeing these beautiful islands is a dream come true, and this guide is the ideal travel companion.

Hawaii is an archipelago consisting of six main islands that are dispersed over the Pacific Ocean. It is known all over the world for its magnificent beauty. A beachfront that is encircled on all sides by verdant jungle and active volcanoes is home to sweeping arches of sugary sand, sweet crescent bay, crescent-shaped bay fluted seacliffs, and turquoise waters. It should come as no surprise that outdoor activities dominate daily life on Hawaii given the state's consistently pleasant weather and breathtaking natural settings. This place is a delight all year round because it has beaches with white sand, restaurants that serve food outside under swaying palm trees, and access to warm waters that are the color of cobalt blue.

The countless villages and cities that dot the landscape of these islands are just as fascinating. In Honolulu, the state capital, you may visit both the historically significant Chinatown as well as the sad site of Pearl Harbor. Other oceanside towns, such as Lhain and Hilo, also offer a variety of delectable cuisine, in addition to fascinating museums and historic places. Hawaii's singular history, which incorporates Polynesian, Asian, and European components, is commemorated through a variety of festivals and dances, including the Chinese New Year, Thanksgiving, and Hawaiian dance. Because of the island's ethnically and racially diverse population, the island's cuisine is a scrumptious fusion of cuisines from around the Pacific Rim.

Where exactly do you start? To make it easier for you to plan the trip of a lifetime to Hawaii's islands, we've broken the state up into its individual islands and written chapters about each one, replete with detailed itineraries, insider tips from residents, and full-color maps. Our Travel Pilots travel book will ensure that you make the most of your time in the archipelago, regardless of how long you decide to stay there. Have a pleasant time reading the book and I hope you enjoy your vacation in Hawaii.

INTRODUCTION ▶ VARIOUS REASONS TO LOVE HAWAII

This remote island is blessed with spectacular natural beauty, a diverse population of species, excellent cuisine, and a wide variety of opportunities to participate in outdoor activities. There is a seemingly endless list of reasons to fall in love with Hawaii; included here are some of our personal favorites.

ARRANGEMENTS WITH MARINE WILDLIFE

In the warm waters that surround Hawaii, majestic whales, honu (green sea turtles), vivid yellow tang fish schools, and beautiful manta rays are just some of the marine life that may be observed.

HONOLULU

The state capital of Hawaii features a variety of hip neighborhoods, delicious fusion cuisine, and a multitude of museums that are both educational and entertaining. It also contains Waikk (p96), which is considered to be one of the most beautiful beaches in the world.

DIFFERENTIATED COASTLINES

Champagne-colored sands, black lava-rock tidal pools, and towering, ridged sea cliffs covered in greenery are just some of the breathtaking sights that can be found along the coast of Hawaii.

THE LŪ'AU

During these traditional feasts, guests are treated to traditional Hawaiian cuisine such as poi (mashed taro root) and haupia (coconut pudding). Additionally, performances of Polynesian music and dancing are provided for the occasion.

VOLCANO LANDSCAPES

The state of Hawaii is home to a number of the world's most active volcanoes, many of which are characterized by desolate lava plains, smoldering craters, and red-hot lava flows, in addition to some of the most breathtaking examples of volcanic beauty.

POKE BOWLS

This traditional Hawaiian dish consists of raw diced fish, typically tuna, that has been marinated in sesame oil and soy sauce, then blended with spring onions and served with rice and other vegetables.

HIKING THE KALALAU TRAIL

This challenging hike traverses jungle paths that hug the edges of cliffs and offers some of the most beautiful views of the Npali Coast State Wilderness Park along the way.

HISTORIC PLACES

There is an incredible variety of historical places to see in Hawaii, ranging from ancient Hawaiian petroglyphs and holy temple complexes to royal palaces and World War II monuments. If you're interested in history, Hawaii is the place to go.

A CUP OF KONA COFFEE

The mineral-rich volcanic slopes of Hawai'i Island are where Kona coffee is grown. This coffee is known for its silky texture, fruity flavor, and hint of smoky spice. It tastes best when it's accompanied by a warm slice of banana bread when served.

A DAY AT THE BEACH

One thing that Hawaii is known for having in abundance is its stunning beaches. The majority of people have a laid-back attitude that makes it easy to relax when sunbathing or while drinking a cocktail at a bar that is located on the beach.

TO HĀNA'S TRAIL

As it makes its way down the edge of Maui's verdant eastern coast, this fabled road takes travelers by a number of breathtaking waterfalls, sandy beaches, and an old temple. You should also prepare yourself for some breathtaking views of the coast.

AWESOME SURFINGS

The ancient Polynesian sport of surfing can be traced back to the islands of the Pacific. The waves here can be anything from a small swell that is perfect for beginners to huge pipes that draw the best surfers in the world.

HAWAII ▶ FAMILIARIZING ONESELF WITH

Hawaii is an archipelago that is located in the middle of the Pacific Ocean and is comprised of over one hundred smaller islands in addition to the six main inhabited islands. Oahu, often known as the "Big Island," is the state's most populous island and the location of Honolulu, the state capital. Hawaii, also known as the "Big Island," is the largest island in the chain.

HAWAII ▶ HONOLULU

Even though it's a very small city, Hawaii's capital on the water delivers quite a punch. This small city is encircled by a dormant volcano and gorgeous hills, and it is divided into two primary areas: the Downtown center and the famed Waikk district. Both of these areas are bordered by a variety of pretty parks, residential neighborhoods, and historic sights.

- The location to go for the most exciting nightlife and the most interesting cultural attractions.
- This area is home to a number of notable landmarks, including Chinatown, Waikiki Beach, the Bishop Museum, and Pearl Harbor.
- Experience At a seaside tavern on Waikk Beach, visitors can get a classic Mai Tai cocktail.

DOWNTOWN HONOLULU AND THE AREA AROUND IT

Chinatown, the Capitol District, and other minor areas make up the relatively distinct sections of downtown, which is composed of tall skyscrapers, serene temples, and artistic museums. The stately 'Iolani Palace is situated in the nearby historic Capitol District, which is home to numerous gastronomic hotspots and galleries of modern art. With its upscale design shops and colorful street paintings, the emerging Kaka'ako district should not be overlooked.

HONOLULU AT MIDNIGHT

There is no better place to find Hawaii's greatest nightlife. The winner is without a doubt Honolulu. You may have a beverage on the beach, sample renowned whiskeys in lavish settings, or sing the night away at a karaoke bar in Honolulu thanks to the city's abundance of hip bars.

The karaoke scene in Honolulu is growing. If you want to be near the beach and have a nice time, go to Wang Chung's (2424 Koa Av) in Waikk. Private rooms as well as delectable Korean snacks and beverages are available at Café Duck Butt in the Kaka'ako neighborhood to keep you going.

Have you been craving a late-night snack? You're in luck because Lucky Belly has a late-night takeout window open Thursday through Saturday from 10 p.m. to 2:30 a.m. that serves delicious ramen noodles. If you're looking for something a little more filling, go to Zippy's (www. zippys.com). This café provides sleepy partygoers Hawaiian comfort food like loco moco (a burger on a bed of rice, topped with an egg and gravy).

Have you had enough of coconut-based drinks? Honolulu's upscale whiskey bars will revitalize your tongue. While the stylish Workplay (www.workplayhi.com), which has a well-curated whiskey collection and live music, is known for its locally distilled spirits and imaginative whiskey cocktails, the quaint Bar Leather Apron is known for its homey atmosphere.

HAWAII ▸ WAIKĪKĪ AND BEYOND

The Waikk neighborhood is well-known for its namesake beach, which stretches from the Ala Wai Canal to the glistening sea. Sunbathers line this long stretch of fine sand, which is bordered by swaying palm trees and hotel beach bars and lapped by tranquil blue waves. On each side of this golden strip, there are even more beaches, including the exquisite Kahanamoku. Just beyond Waikk Beach lies the hopping Kalkaua Avenue, which parallels Waikk Beach and is lined with posh shops, great dining establishments, and chic condos. To the west, in the Ala Moana neighborhood, there is a sizable retail mall and a well-liked park.

BEYOND THE CENTER

The Ko'olau Range's rainforest-covered peaks and valleys to the north, Diamond Head's volcanic crater to the east, and the Punchbowl crater to the west all encircle the city. Between this natural beauty and the city center lie the superbly decorated Queen Emma Summer Palace, the verdant Lyon Arboretum, and the fascinating Bishop Museum. On the western shore of the city is Pearl Harbor, a national memorial renowned for its moving monuments and museums.

HAWAII ▶ O'AHU

O'ahu is the third-largest island in the archipelago, covering an area of 600 square miles (1,550 square kilometers). It was created by two volcanoes, the Ko'olau Range and the Wai'anae Mountains in the northeast and west, respectively. Around AD 1,200–1,300, travelers started arriving on O'ahu from a number of other South Pacific islands, notably Tahiti and the Marquesas Islands of today. The earliest people were drawn to the island's resource-rich edge, where they built communities.

HAWAII ▶ HANAUMA BAY

Hanauma Bay's distinctive morphology was created 32,000 years ago by a succession of powerful volcanic eruptions. The shallow, sandy bottom of the sheltering bay, which is now a flooded crater, is dotted with fragile coral and dark basalt rock, making it the ideal habitat for marine life. This area is home to more than 400 different species of vibrant fish, as well as green sea turtles, moray eels, and the occasional curious spinner dolphin or manta ray. The area is a fantastic place to snorkel, especially for novices, due to its calm waters and abundance of marine life. On this beach, there are also restrooms, a snack bar, and a location where you may rent snorkeling gear.

Hanauma has gained so much notoriety as a travel destination that the state has been forced to take measures to protect it from overtourism. There is a $3 entrance fee, cash only, a cap on daily visitors at 1,000, and there are only 300 parking places available. All visitors must view a nine-minute orientation movie before they can enter the park, which is shown at the bay's acclaimed Marine Education Center.

LOVELY SEASCAPE
For a breathtaking view, drive to the parking lot perched over Hanauma Bay. From here, you can see the coral reef, half-moon beach, and gorgeous blue water in its entirety.

MARINE LIFE SPECIES
marine turtles, green The honu (green sea turtles) of Hawaii are the largest hardshelled sea turtles in the world and a threatened species.

PARROTFISH
These vibrant fish can be recognized by their distinctive, parrot-like beak of fused teeth.

FISH FROM THE MORAY
These grumpy fish, which are typical to Hawaii, like to hide in crevices in rocks and coral. Be cautious since they have teeth.

YELLOW TANGO
The brightly colored yellow tang is the simplest to identify of all the Hawaiian reef fish.

THE REEF'S TRIGGERFISH
The fish that serves as Hawaii's official state fish is called Humuhumunukunukuapua'a in Hawaiian.

CRATER KOKO

On a projecting headland, the volcanic Koko Crater rises to a height of 1,200 feet (366 m). Within the basin lies the Koko Crater Botanical Garden, which has a variety of uncommon, drought-tolerant, and endangered plant species from all over the world. The gardens are accessible by a 2-mile (3-kilometer) informative circular path, or you can join a guided tour led by a horticultural specialist. Only scheduled visits are permitted; to schedule a visit, call (808) 768-7135.

Beyond the crater, one can attempt the more challenging Koko Head Stairs walk, which follows a former, steep train track and provides panoramic views.

POINT MAKAPU'U

The island of O'ahu's farthest eastern tip, Makapu'u Point, offers stunning views of the ocean, seabird sanctuaries of Rabbit and Kohikaipu, as well as the rugged shoreline. The Makapu'u Lighthouse is a great location for whale watching in the winter.

A remote cove next to Makapu'u Beach has some of the strongest bodysurfing waves on the island, but it takes skill and precise timing to avoid getting dragged onto the rocks.

Though there are hiking routes that go up into the Black Mountains, you just need to go around 100 feet to get some great pictures (30 meters).

TEMPLE OF BYODO-IN

This reconstruction of a 950-year-old Japanese temple cannot be seen from the road. The only indication is a sign for a historical site from the Hawai'i Visitors & Convention Bureau. After turning into the Valley of Temples, a non-denominational cemetery, the road winds into the valley to reach this hidden gem, its walls scarlet against fluted, green hills. Before approaching the shrine, which is guarded by a 9-foot (3-meter) gold and lacquer Buddha, take off your shoes.
Visit the temple at dusk for a serene experience. Since the temple closes at five o'clock, you won't be able to see the Buddha, but you will be able to enjoy the great silence, broken only by the singing of birds.

RANCH KUALOA

In 1850, an American doctor paid King Kamehameha III $1,300 to acquire Kualoa Ranch. Today, the ranch serves as both a working cattle ranch and a day trip for tourists eager to experience the way of life of a paniolo (a Hawaiian cowboy).
The vast bulk of operations take place in the two main areas, Ka'a'awa Valley and Hakipuu Valley. A well-liked activity is the guided movie tour, which leads tourists through the stunning Ka'a'awa Valley, sometimes known as Hollywood's "Hawaii Backlot," to see the filming locations used in more than 50 Hollywood blockbusters and TV shows, including Jurassic Park and Lost. A historic Hawaiian fishpond and a private beach are accessible only by boat in Hakipuu Valley. Other options include horseback riding, ATV excursions, and an electric mountain bike tour. It is advisable to plan excursions far in advance because the ranch is well-liked.

TRAILS OF THE HULA

Three trails in the Hau'ula Trails area—the Hau'ula Loop Trail, Ma'akua Ridge Trail, and Ma'akua Gulch Trail—provide hikers the best of what Hawaii has to offer. They are spacious, stable, and offer breathtaking views of the valley.
ocean and mountains. Any of the pathways, which all start just beyond the little settlement of Hau'ula, off Hau'ula Homestead Road, beyond the end of Ma'akua Road, should take around two hours to accomplish a round-trip.

HALE'IWA

Formerly a hippie hangout and little plantation village, Hale'iwa is now a well-liked North Shore surfing location. A single main street in the town is lined with restaurants, coffee shops, boutiques, grocery stores, and art galleries, giving it a bohemian feel.

Public beaches that have recently been maintained line a stunning boat harbor. The nearby Hale'iwa Beach Park, which is guarded by a breakwater, is one of the few places on the North Shore where swimming in the winter is typically safe, despite Ali'i Beach Park's reputation for big waves and surfing competitions.

The hamlet is well-known for its annual Obon Festival, which features the Eddie Aikau Big Wave Invitational at Waimea Bay. Folk dancing and the release of hundreds of floating lanterns into the water are part of the event, which is held each summer at a Buddhist temple on the water.

When traveling west from Hale'iwa, you'll pass through Waialua, past a former sugar plantation, and arrive in Mokul'ia, where lonely white-sand beaches meet polo fields. You can enjoy a pleasant afternoon here watching parachutists from the nearby Dillingham Airfield descend across the water like clouds of vibrant butterflies.

PARK AT 'EHUKAI BEACH

The rocky coastline of 'Ehukai Beach Park is surrounded by vast stretches of sand, and the surf is raging there. The most well-known surfing spot in this area is the tubular Banzai Pipeline, which produces waves with incredible steepness and strength, some of which reach heights of over 30 feet (9 m). The name Banzai, which derives from the war cry of Japanese kamikaze pilots, was first given to these waves during the narration of the late 1950s movie Surf Safari.

Lifeguards at the beach are kept very busy due to the treacherous ocean bottom and the allure of massive winter surf; summer waves are more moderate but may still be too dangerous for inexperienced surfers. Sunbathers who visit the beach park to take advantage of the soft sand and picnic areas are also drawn there.

CENTER FOR POLYNESIAN CULTURE

Mormon missionaries established the town of L'ie in 1864 following an unsuccessful attempt to settle on the island of Lna'i. The Polynesian Cultural Center, a significant educational theme park that is one of O'ahu's most well-known attractions, is currently housed at L'ie along with a Mormon temple, a campus of Brigham Young University, and other buildings. Students from the Pacific region, including those from Fiji, Tongan, Hawaiian, Samoan, Tahitian, and Mori, exhibit their arts and crafts and dance in six Polynesian "villages" at the venue (Aotearoa). The instruction, whether it be on Tongan drumming or Samoan firemaking, is given in practically continuous minishows, with audience participation encouraged. There is also a theater showing a variety of movies.

The afternoon event Huki: A Canoe Celebration incorporates legends from all around the islands together with performances of singing, dancing, and martial arts in doublehulled canoes. H-Breath of Life, the evening show, offers Polynesian music and dance in addition to fireknife dancing. A fun l'au show including a delectable buffet of Polynesian foods like Kalua pork and lomi-lomi salmon salad (raw, salted salmon minced with tomatoes and onions) or a sumptuous prime rib buffet can also be scheduled by tourists.

THE WAIMEA VALLEY

One of the few ahupua'a, or Hawaiian land divisions that extend from mountain to sea, still exists in this lush valley. Since it is a stunning, natural setting, it is a sacred place for Hawaiians and a significant educational resource.

The valley was previously a destination for tourists to enjoy lavish hula performances, and afterwards the Audubon Society used it as a facility (a bird conservation group). This lovely valley is presently under the control of the Office of Hawaiian Affairs. Among the features are a waterfall, a 5,000-plant botanical collection, a wildlife refuge, and historic remains, including a heiau (temple) dedicated to Lono, the god of harmony, agriculture, and music, built in the fifteenth century. Walking tours and cultural activities like lei-making, hula lessons, and storytelling are all included in the admission price. Additionally, as the park provides fantastic opportunities for birdwatching, it is advisable to carry binoculars.

Cross the street to Waimea Beach Park after your visit to go swimming or snorkeling.

COAST OF WAI'ANAE

Due to its remote location and rough shoreline, which is made up of some of the island's oldest lava, O'ahu's bright Leeward coast continues to draw few visitors. It's a good idea to stock up on supplies at Wai'anae's major town, which is also called Wai'anae. One of the most stunning beaches on the coast is Pka' Bay, where a barrier conceals an azure lagoon with sand that feels like silk under your feet. About 3 miles (5 kilometers) away lies Mauna Lahilahi, a tiny mountain rising only 230 feet (70 meters) to the northwest. Ancient temple ruins and petroglyphs on its eastern side depicting characters that resemble humans and dogs make it a sacred Hawaiian location that has been revered for millennia. A little further north, Mkaha Beach is renowned for its massive surf. Kne'k Heiau, in the Mkaha Valley, has ki'i and thatched dwellings (carved idols). It was used as a battle temple by Kamehameha I. The name "mkaha" in Hawaiian means "ferocious," and robbers used to frequent this valley.

PLANTATION VILLAGE IN HAWAII

In an outdoor setting, Hawaii's Plantation Village, which cost $3 million to rebuild, presents more than 100 years of life on a sugar plantation. A common pidgin language developed despite plantation owners dividing workers along ethnic lines, as seen in the excellent presentation.
Among the recreated structures from the various ethnic communities who worked the farms are Korean, Puerto Rican, and Japanese homes, as well as a Japanese bathhouse, Chinese cookhouse, and a Shinto shrine. Personal belongings are arranged in the homes to give the impression that the residents have just left.

POINT KA'ENA

On O'ahu's westernmost tip, Ka'ena Point offers a rocky, steep shoreline with breathtaking sunsets. The point is accessible via a strenuous but short 2-mile (3-kilometer) trek.
The rock off the point is said to be a portion of Kaua'i that the mythical Maui stole while seeking to unite the two islands. On clear days, Kaua'i can be seen to the north. Also visible are humpback whales, green turtles, and rare monk seals. Here, the biggest waves in the world crash against the rocks, yet surfing is not advised. The closest highways are Highway 93 and Highway 930. The two roads are not interconnected.

CRATER IN KA'AU

Three volcanic craters (tuff cones) can be reached by car from Honolulu: the well-known Diamond Head Crater, the exposed Koko Crater, and the less well-known Ka'au Crater. Unlike the first two, you cannot drive up to the Ka'au Crater, but there is a lovely, challenging trek that leads to the sluggish crater caldera and crater rim.
The eight-kilometer (five-mile) trek starts at the back of Palolo Valley and circles around while traversing thick forests and by three breathtaking waterfalls. The stunning panoramic views of the Windward side of O'ahu, including Olomana, N Mokulua, and Mokoli'i, make the tough climb (which necessitates scrambling up muddy and slippery rocks) well worth it.

HAWAII ▸ MOLOKAʻI AND LĀNAʻI

MOLOKAʻI

Together with Lnaʻi and Kahoʻolawe, Molokaʻi is made up of two extinct volcanoes that were once connected to Maui. On the island's protected southern slopes, where they grew vegetables along the shoreline and raised fish in rocky cages just offshore, the majority of the inhabitants lived. Although Molokaʻi was repeatedly conquered by troops from Oʻahu, Maui, and Hawaiʻi Island in the 1500s, its native religious leaders, particularly the heavenly prophet Lanikaula, helped the island develop a reputation for spiritual strength. In 1795, Kamehameha I invaded Molokaʻi as part of his campaign to unite the Hawaiian Islands. In the 1860s, his grandson Kamehameha V built a vacation home nearby and planted more than a thousand coconut trees, some of which may still be seen in the Kapuaiwa Coconut Grove today. Under his rule, the Kalaupapa Peninsula on the island was recognized as a leprosarium.

Lnaʻi was not one of the Polynesian-populated Hawaiian islands, despite the fact that many of them were because of their reputation for being haunted by evil spirits. After breaching a kapu law on Maui in the 1500s, the island's first occupant, a man by the name of Kauluaau, was exiled there. Like the other Hawaiian Islands, Lnaʻi was administered by Kamehameha I in the 1790s, who used it as a vacation destination for fishermen. Lnaʻi was bought by James Dole, head of the Hawaiian Pineapple Company (later the Dole Company), in 1922, and became the largest pineapple plantation in the world. Seventy years after pineapple harvesting stopped, the Castle & Cooke Corporation (Dole's parent company) built two upscale hotels nearby. In 2012, the majority of Lnaʻi was sold to American billionaire Larry Ellison, who is turning it into an eco-friendly vacation spot.

LĀNA'I

Sun-baked Lna'i, previously the biggest pineapple plantation in the world, was owned by the Dole Company. In 1991, the Castle & Cooke Corporation (Dole's parent company) built two opulent resorts and rehired island farm workers as hotel staff. This change in identity made it possible for tourists to visit and explore the island's numerous beaches, cliffs, and historic sites. In 2012, software tycoon Larry Ellison purchased 98 percent of the island and implemented several eco-friendly and sustainability-oriented changes.

NATIONAL HISTORICAL PARK OF KALAUPAPA

The Kalaupapa Peninsula was initially a community for people with Hansen's Disease and is secluded from the rest of Moloka'i by a wall of gigantic rocks (leprosy). The sad remains of this far-off town are still visible in the park today.

The Kalaupapa Peninsula was designated as a leper colony and those who had contracted the disease were sent here after it became apparent that leprosy had been imported and was threatening the Hawaiian people's survival in 1865. The main settlement was in the village of Kalawao, which was on the peninsula's eastern edge. Many patients decided to stay on the peninsula even after the policy of mandatory isolation was discontinued in 1969 due to new treatment that rendered patients non-contagious.

A handful of the original patients still voluntarily reside in the area, which is now a national park, serving as a memorial. The village is made up of four churches and almost 200 other historic buildings; many of the wood-frame houses from the 1920s were built in the Hawaiian Plantation style. Additionally, there is a lighthouse that houses one of the Pacific's most potent lighthouses. You can only visit this peaceful village and the neighboring tranquil seashore park as part of an organized tour, which must be scheduled in advance.

You may reach the park via plane, walking, or taking a mule ride along the Kalaupapa Pali Trail (permit required). The 26 switchbacks that wound their way down cliffs during this strenuous walk offer panoramic vistas of the peninsula. Currently, the trail is closed because of a landslide.

IMPORTANT DETAILS

BEFORE YOU DEPART

It is important to be well prepared in advance of your trip in order to get the most out of the experience. Think about the following things before you leave on your trip to make sure that you are ready for everything that can happen.

VISAS AND PASSPORTS

For information on entry requirements, including visas, contact the US Department of State or the consulate of the United States in your country. Canadian visitors to the United States are required to provide a passport in order to get entry. Citizens of the 39 countries that participate in the US Visa Waiver Program, including the United Kingdom, are exempt from the requirement to obtain a visa in order to enter the United States for stays of up to 90 days; however, they are required to apply for the Electronic System for Travel Authorization (ESTA) in advance and have a valid passport. Other travelers will be required to present both a passport and a tourist visa in order to gain entry. You are required to have a round-trip airplane ticket in order to enter the United States.

THE OFFICIAL COUNSEL OF THE GOVERNMENT

It is essential to get advice from both yourself and the government of the United States before going on a trip. The Department of State in the United States, the Department of Foreign and Commonwealth Office in the United Kingdom, the Australian Department of Foreign Affairs and Trade, and Hawaii's Safe Travels all have the most up-to-date information regarding health, safety, and the regulations that are specific to the area.

DETAILS PERTAINING TO CUSTOMS

Go Hawaii, the state's official tourism board, is a good resource for information on the regulations that control the products and currencies that can be brought into and taken out of the state.
Never take any part of the natural environment back with you, especially not sand, coral, or lava rocks.

INSURANCE

We strongly suggest that you acquire an all-inclusive insurance plan that includes protection against theft, loss of things, medical care, cancellations, and delays. Additionally, we advise that you read the policy's fine print very thoroughly. Due to the absence of a national health care system in the United States, the cost of receiving medical treatment might be prohibitively high for visitors visiting Hawaii. Verify that your health insurance policy from the mainland covers you while you're here in Hawaii.

VACCINATIONS

Consult government instructions for specifics on COVID-19 immunization requirements. If you are traveling from or have been in a region that is experiencing an outbreak of a disease that requires vaccination, such as cholera or yellow fever, you are not obliged to have any additional vaccinations.

MONEY

Cards, both credit and debit, including contactless cards, can be used to complete the vast majority of large transactions. There are a lot of automated teller machines (ATMs), so it shouldn't be difficult for travelers to get cash using their standard credit cards. Always keep some cash with you in case you need it for things like roadside stands, tips, or businesses that only accept cash.
Tipping is a common practice. Waiters and bartenders typically receive $1 per drink or 15–20 percent of the total cost, respectively. When using a cab, you should anticipate to pay an additional 10%–15% of the fare. Housekeepers should be paid between $2 and $5 per day, and luggage handlers should be paid between $1 and $2 each bag.

THE MAKING OF ACCOMMODATIONS RESERVATIONS

There is a diverse selection of places to stay in Hawaii, ranging from opulent resorts to quaint hotels. Camping is often a good choice for people who are trying to save money. The Christmas holiday season, the summer (particularly June to August), and spring break are the periods of year with the highest volume of customers, and prices rise as a direct result of this increased demand. Make your reservations as far in advance as possible to save money.
In regions such as Waikk, there is a hotel tax that is 10.25 percent, in addition to potential resort fees that are $25 per day and parking costs that are $20 per day.

SPECIFIC REQUIREMENTS TRAVELERS

The majority of hotels, restaurants, and tourist destinations have wheelchair ramps, places dedicated specifically for handicap parking, and other accessible services. A regular occurrence is the translation of important signs into Braille. On the website of the Disability and Communication Access Board, there are factsheets that may be downloaded regarding the accessibility of parks, beaches, and other attractions.
At both Pearl Harbor and Haleakala National Park, visitors have access to park pamphlets and signage in braille, sites and locations that are accessible to wheelchair users, and the possibility to employ interpreters who are fluent in American Sign Language (ASL). There are various beaches in Hawaii that have all-terrain wheelchairs available for rent; for additional information, check the Go Hawaii website.

LANGUAGE

Both English and Hawaiian, also known as 'lelo Hawai'i, are recognized as official languages in the state of Hawaii, making it the only state in the United States to do so. Although the number of people who are proficient in the latter language is increasing, just about 0.1 percent of Hawaii's population speaks it fluently.

WHEN WE'RE OPEN AND CLOSED

On Mondays, a great number of restaurants and institutions are closed. The majority of financial institutions are closed on Sundays, while the majority of other companies and tourist sites only open in the afternoon. Celebrations throughout the State Many places of interest and companies keep irregular or limited hours, and the vast majority of establishments are shut down on Christmas Day and New Year's Day.

HOW TO GET AROUND IN THE AREA

Find out how to get to where you're going and travel like a pro, regardless of whether you're just going to one island or the entire archipelago.

TRAVELING VIA AIR

The Honolulu International Airport, which is situated 10 miles (16 kilometers) to the west of the city of Honolulu on the island of O'ahu, serves as the primary transportation hub for the state of Hawaii. It has three terminals, and those terminals handle domestic, international, and interisland flights respectively. Maui's Kahului Airport, Hawai'i Island's Ellison Onizuka Kona International Airport, and Kauai's Lhu'e Airport are not the only airports that accept long-haul and interisland flights as landing destinations.
The West Coast of the United States serves as the departure point for the majority of the nonstop flights that connect the continental United States to Hawaii. A stopover on the West Coast is common for flights to Hawaii departing from other parts of North America (including Canada) and the United States.
There are many airlines that fly from Europe to Hawaii, and some of them make stops in the continental United States and Canada along the trip. United Carriers and Air Canada are just two examples of such carriers. Both Qantas and Air New Zealand operate direct flights to Honolulu from the cities of Sydney, Australia and Auckland, New Zealand.

THE JOURNEY THERE WILL BE VIA SEA.

Norwegian Cruise Line offers itineraries that take passengers around Hawaii for an entire week. This port is home port for a number of high-end cruise lines, including Royal Caribbean.

TRAVELING BETWEEN ISLANDS

Flying between the islands is a straightforward and hassle-free option, and there is a wide variety of connections available; but, the costs can add up. The most popular airlines that provide service between the islands are Hawaiian Airlines, Southwest Airlines, and Mokulele Airlines. Interisland flights are available from the principal airports on Oahu, Maui, Hawai'i Island, and Kaua'i. These airports, along with Hilo International Airport on Hawai'i Island and Kapalua Airport on Maui, make up the entire network. Only flights from Honolulu International Airport, Maui's Kahului and Kapalua airports, and Honolulu International Airport or Kahului Airport service Lna'i Airport. Moloka'i Airport can only be reached by flights departing from Honolulu International Airport or Kahului Airport.

TRAVEL VIA FERRY BETWEEN THE ISLANDS

The only inter-island ferry service in Hawaii is run by Interisland Ferry Travel Expeditions, and it travels between Maui's Lhain Harbor and Lana'i's Manele Harbor. The trip takes around one hour to complete, and there are multiple departures every day; during the winter months, the excursion doubles as a whale-watching cruise. A ticket may be purchased for a starting price of $30 for an adult and $20 for a child.

TRANSPORTATION PROVIDED BY THE CITY.

On Oahu, TheBus is the most comprehensive of the islands' comprehensive public transportation systems, which also include Maui Bus, Kauai Bus, and Hawai'i Island's Hele-On Bus. On their own websites, each of these companies provides details regarding safety and cleanliness, as well as timetables, information regarding tickets, and transit maps. On the island of Oahu, the city of Honolulu has a trolley system, and they are now building a rail system. On the islands of Moloka'i and Lna'i, there is no public transportation; as a result, car rentals are essential, and the only other transportation options are shuttle buses and taxis.

BUSES

TheBus provides service to a significant portion of Oahu, with multiple routes terminating at the airport. On the bus, you can pay with cash in exact change or a reloadable HOLO card for a one-way journey (which costs $2.75), a one-day fare (which costs $5.50), or a monthly pass (which costs $70.00). The latter option is a smart alternative to go with if you intend to make frequent use of TheBus. You can get free HOLO cards that can be filled at local companies including 7-Elevens and ABC Stores, as well as online. You can also get a bus pass at TheBus Pass Office.
This article is about the free and helpful application DaBus2, which displays TheBus schedules and routes.
On Maui, there are 14 separate routes that are serviced by the Maui Bus. These routes serve the western half of the island, where most of the major cities and attractions are located. On the bus, tickets can only be purchased using physical currency (exact change). The fee for a ride in one direction is $2, while the price for the day is $4. Every day, bus service operates between the hours of around 7 a.m. and 9 p.m., but the schedule varies depending on the route.

The Kauai Bus travels along the major island road in its entirety, beginning in Hanalei in the north and ending in Kekaha in the west. It operates on an hourly basis Monday through Saturday, but there are fewer services available on Sunday. On board, passengers must have the exact amount of cash in their possession to purchase a ticket. A ticket for one-way travel costs $2, while a ticket for the day costs $5.
Kailua-Kona is linked to the Kohala resorts as well as Hilo and Hawai'i Volcanoes National Park on the island of Hawaii by means of the Hele-On Bus, which also travels between Kailua-Kona and Hilo by way of Waimea and Honoka'a. Only cash can be accepted for the purchase of bus tickets on board the vehicle (precise change). Every ride will cost a total of $2, which is a flat rate. Although the timings are not optimal for taking in the local attractions, they do offer good value for the money.

TROLLEYS

The open-air trams that run all throughout Honolulu on Oahu are a remarkable mode of transportation that can be seen all over the city. Waikk Trolley is the company that runs all three routes, which take passengers to Chinatown and other historic places (on the red line), Diamond Head and seashore viewpoints (on the green/blue line), and shopping centers (on the green/blue line) (pink line). Tickets can be purchased offline at tour desks or online at several websites. Day passes are available for purchase on all lines, with the pink line's pass costing $5 and the red, green/blue, and orange lines each costing $25. There are other options for all-line tickets valid for 1, 4, or 7 days.

TRAIN

The Honolulu Rail Transit project, which has been in the works for a considerable amount of time, will involve the construction of a rail system that will cover a distance of 20 miles (32 kilometers) and connect the airport and the city. The initial stage of the project is scheduled to get underway in 2022, and it is anticipated that the full network would be finished in 2027.

TAXIS

Taxis can be found at all major airports, as well as in the front of all large hotels and most big retail centers. Outside of Honolulu, it is often faster to go to a taxi stand or phone ahead to schedule a pick-up than it is to try to hail a cab on the street. In some more remote locations, access to taxi service is limited or nonexistent altogether. Both Uber and Lyft, two of the most well-known apps for hailing rides, are accessible in major cities.

DRIVING

Even though Honolulu has the worst traffic congestion of any large city in the United States, driving in Hawaii is typically a pleasant experience, and it is frequently an excellent way to get around and explore the islands. Because residents of the area are typically not in a hurry, you should plan your excursions so that you have plenty of time. Check your mirrors frequently and move over to the shoulder when necessary to let other vehicles pass on narrow roads because locals never use their horns unless there is an urgent situation. Always check the weather prediction before heading out, since heavy rain could cause roads to become flooded and unsafe to travel during or after the storm.
If you ask a local for directions, they will frequently provide you with landmarks to use as reference points. Around Honolulu, you'll hear people saying "Go ewa" (northwest) or "Go diamondhead" (southeast). On the other islands, you'll hear people saying "mauka" (toward the mountain) and "makai" (toward the sea) (toward the sea).

AUTOMOBILE RENTAL

If you want to hire a car in Hawaii, you need to be at least 21 years old (surcharges may apply for those under 25). All drivers are required to have a passport, a credit card, and a valid driver's license. Additionally, drivers whose licenses are not in English are required to have an International Driving Permit. Large rental firms are represented at the airports on each of the four main islands by their own desks. They offer vehicles of every size; nevertheless, in order to operate a 4WD vehicle, you may need the assistance of a specialist. It is typically not difficult to rent a car in Waikk for a day or two, but in other places, you will need to make extensive preparations in advance.
The vast majority of customers opt to purchase a Loss Damage Waiver for an extra price (LDW). This protects you from Hawaii's "no fault" policy, which makes the driver responsible for any damage to a rental automobile regardless of who was at fault for the accident. Always check to see whether your insurance policy or credit card will cover any damage done to the rental car you have reserved. The vast majority of car rental businesses do not permit driving on muddy roads.

Parking A lot of hotels provide free parking for their guests, and a lot of the larger hotels and restaurants also have valet parking services. With one notable exception, hotels and parking lots in Waikk can charge upwards of $20 for overnight parking fees. Before booking a reservation, you should first determine whether or not parking is included.

Free parking in Honolulu is in high demand, especially on the weekends, so spots go quickly. You also have the choice of parking in garages or at street meters; if you go with the latter, be sure to have enough of cash on hand, and bear in mind that parking at street meters is typically free on Sundays. Pay close attention to any and all parking signs in order to avoid getting a penalty or having your vehicle hauled away.

THE PRINCIPLES OF SAFE DRIVING

Always drive on the right side of the road, only passing in the left lane when necessary, and always yield to oncoming vehicles coming from the right. Drivers are required to defer to pedestrians whenever they are crossing the roadway, even if they are doing so illegally. Seat belts are mandatory for every passenger in the front and back of the vehicle. Texting while behind the wheel is against the law, but drivers are allowed to use hands-free devices when talking on the phone. The maximum speed limit in Hawaii is one of the lowest in the United States, and there are signs all across the state that make the limit as well as the enforcement of it very evident.

It is illegal in the state of Hawaii to operate a motor vehicle while under the influence of alcohol or drugs, as well as to have open containers of alcoholic beverages in a moving vehicle. The maximum amount of alcohol that can legally be present in a person's blood is 0.08 %. (0.02 percent for drivers under 21). Driving under the influence of alcohol can result in fines and/or jail time.

CYCLING

Paths suitable for bicycling may be found everywhere on the islands, but the islands' jaw-dropping scenery also comes with its share of challenges. There are a few things that you need to be aware of, such as the weather, the amount of traffic, and the routes that are extremely congested.
In metropolitan areas, continual efforts are being made to improve the safety of cyclists. From Moiliili to Downtown Honolulu, the entirety of South King Street has been converted into a protected bike lane for cyclists. However, a travel taken at a leisurely pace could be disrupted by heavy traffic. To get out of the city before they begin pedaling, many cyclists utilize TheBus' frontloading bike racks, which are available at no additional fee. On the other islands, too, you can find a great deal of spectacular biking terrain to explore. The Kauai Trail is a shared cycling and walking path that runs along the east coast of Kauai for a total distance of 7 miles (11 kilometers). On the island of Maui, cyclists flock to the breathtaking 25-mile (40-kilometer) ride down Haleakala (p160). There is also a family-friendly, carfree trail between Kahului and P'ia on the island's north shore that connects Kahului and P'ia. Mana Road on Hawai'i Island is a dirt path that spans 40 miles (64 kilometers) and is located high on the slopes of Mauna Kea. Brave mountain cyclists travel there (p194). There is noticeably less vehicular traffic on the roadways of Moloka'i and Lna'i compared to the roads of the other Hawaiian islands, making them ideal for cycling. Additionally, there are many side roads and dirt pathways to explore on both islands.

BIKE RENTALS AND BIKE SHARING

Programs for the shared use of bicycles are offered on both Oahu and Hawai'i Island. Biki is a bike sharing company that operates in Honolulu. They have 1,300 bikes and 130 docking stations spread out over the city. Bikeshare Hawaii Island, which has locations in both Kona and Hilo, also provides bikesharing services, albeit on a much more limited scale. There are numerous places to rent bicycles across the islands, and the majority of these places have a selection of bicycles available for rent, including road bikes, mountain bikes, and electric bikes.

HIKING AND WALKING

Downtown districts that are accessible on foot can be found in all of Hawaii's major cities and towns. Waikk, Chinatown, and Kaka'ako are just a few of the neighborhoods in Honolulu that are easily navigable on foot. The city also features a number of pedestrian gardens and parks throughout its various neighborhoods. In addition, there are a variety of walks in the surrounding area, one of which is the stunning Diamond Head crater path.

Outside of the towns and cities, there are many opportunities for hiking around the islands, particularly in the national parks. Hike through a volcanic landscape at Hawai'i Volcanoes National Park, through a rainforest at Waimea Canyon and Kke'e State Parks, or take on the Kalalau Trail in Npali Coast State Wilderness Park, which is widely regarded as one of the most breathtaking coastline hikes in the world.

A FEW TRAVEL TIPS

In Hawaii, a small amount of familiarity with the local culture can go a very long way. You won't need to look anywhere else during your stay because you'll discover all the helpful hints and information that you require right here.

PROTECTION FOR ONESELF

The state of Hawaii is known for having a low rate of violent crime, making it an excellent destination for tourists. If you apply some basic reasoning to a situation, you should not have too many problems. The most likely event is that something was stolen from a rented vehicle. Never risk losing valuables by leaving them in the vehicle, as criminals are skilled at picking the locks on doors and trunks. In spite of the fact that the rate of crime in Honolulu is not nearly as high as it is in some other major cities in the United States, the capital of Hawaii has its fair share of sleazy areas. If you are traveling late at night, ask the concierge of your hotel for recommendations on where to go. It is against the law to hitchhike, and going on walks by yourself is not a good idea because of the risk of becoming disoriented or being involved in an accident.

Hawaii is the only state in the United States that does not have a single police department that covers the entire state. Instead, each county — or island, to put it another way — is responsible for its own independent police force. Report anything that has been stolen to the police station that is closest to you within the next day, and bring some form of identification with you when you go. Get a copy of the police report before filing an insurance claim for the damages. Get in touch with your country's embassy if your passport is lost or stolen, or if you are engaged in a serious accident or crime. The people who live in Hawaii, as a whole, are generally very accepting of others, regardless of their ethnicity, gender, or sexual orientation. The decision to consider making same-sex marriage legal was made public in 2013 in the state of Hawaii, which was the first state in the United States to even consider the possibility. The local LGBTQ+ community frequents Queen's Surf Beach, which is located on Waikkk Beach and is part of Waikkk Beach. LGBTQ+-friendly hotels, restaurants, and clubs may be found throughout Honolulu, notably in the Waikkk neighborhood.

PROTECTION AND WELLNESS

Hawaii, while being in a tropical location, does not present many health risks. The most significant threats are ultraviolet radiation from the sun and saltwater from the ocean. Put on a hat, some sunglasses, and sunscreen that is reef-safe in order to shield your eyes from the sun's powerful rays. Keep in mind that it is illegal to sell sunblock in Hawaii that contains the reef-damaging ingredients oxybenzone and octinoxate. Consume a lot of water and try to avoid going outside when the sun is at its hottest or when the temperature is particularly high for extended periods of time.

When you are swimming in the water, regardless of how much experience you have, you should always pay close attention to the conditions. During the summer months, many beaches have calm waters, but during the winter months, the waves can be dangerous. It is not recommended that someone who has never surfed before attempt it without first receiving adequate instruction. Always be sure to ask lifeguards about the current conditions, and make sure to observe any written warnings. There are typically lifeguards stationed at the more popular beaches. Be very careful if you go to beaches that aren't being watched by lifeguards, especially if you don't know how to recognize potentially dangerous currents. You can obtain additional information by going to the website for Hawaii Beach Safety, which features up-to-date information on the conditions of the wind and the current.

There is a possibility of encountering scorpions in the desert; the jungle, on the other hand, is home to centipedes and mosquitoes; and the ocean is home to box jellyfish and Portuguese man-of-war.

TOBACCO, ALCOHOLIC BEVERAGES, AND ILLICIT NARCOTICS.

It is against the law to light up in any public location, which includes stores, theaters, nightclubs, bars, and restaurants. This rule also applies to electronic cigarettes. People above the age of 21 are legally permitted to purchase tobacco products.
The minimum age to purchase alcohol in most states is 21 years old. It is against the law to consume alcohol in a state or national park, and it is also against the law to have an open container of alcohol in your car.
Possession of up to 0.1 ounce (3 grams) of cannabis might result in a modest fine being levied against the individual. Marijuana possession in larger quantities, like with other illegal substances, is against the law and can result in severe penalties or even incarceration if the offender is found guilty.

ID

When traveling to Hawaii, tourists should always have some form of identification on them at all times. In addition to being required to present identification in order to enter Hawaii and move between the islands, you'll also need it in order to make hotel reservations, demonstrate that you are of legal age to purchase alcoholic beverages and cigarettes, and rent a vehicle, a watersport, or a bicycle.

THE REGION'S CUSTOMS PROCEDURES

Because residents of the area are typically not in a rush, you should plan to go at a leisurely pace and only use your horn in an urgent situation. Sandals, sneakers, shorts, and comfortable apparel for evenings out should all be packed for the trip. Always take off your shoes at the door of a private residence before entering. Because these shirts are not just for tourists but are also worn frequently by locals, we should refer to them as aloha shirts rather than Hawaiian shirts. Aloha means "aloha" in Hawaiian. In Hawaii, it is illegal to trespass on private property. When you are out touring the island, keep an eye out for signs that say "kapu," which means "forbidden" and typically means "do not trespass."
Before visiting private property, you should always inquire with the owners for permission. Every one of the beaches is accessible to the general public.

PLACES OF WORSHIP AND UNSPOILED NATURE TO EXPLORE

When you are in natural areas or sacred sites, you are not allowed to take any rocks, sand, or other natural resources with you; in fact, you are not even allowed to move the rocks. Follow routes that are well designated, pay attention to and observe any signs, and stay off of any structures that you see. Always throw trash away in the containers designated for that purpose, or bring it with you when you leave.

WI-FI NETWORKS AND MOBILE PHONES

A great number of cafes and bars offer free WiFi to their customers, however the vast majority of hotels charge a daily fee for WiFi access in the guest rooms.
If you want to use your cellular phone while you're in Hawaii, you should get in touch with your phone carrier in advance. Local Subscriber Identifier (SIM) cards are available for purchase from T-Mobile, Verizon, and other operators of cellular phone networks. Although cell phone coverage is typically very good in resort and metropolitan areas, it is possible that it will be inconsistent or even nonexistent in more remote spots. In the event of a critical situation, hikers in particular should not rely on their mobile phones for assistance.

POST

The United States Postal Service (USPS) offers a dependable and cost-effective service, and it has branches in most of the main cities. The standard fees charged by the United States Postal Service are applicable, although the delivery time of the mail may be extended.

BOTH TAXES AND REFUNDS

There is a sales tax of 4% applied to all goods and services, and there may be additional county levies of up to 0.7% added on top of that. You'll also need to factor in the cost of any applicable hotel taxes. Tax refunds are not available to travellers from other countries.

CARDS OFFERING SAVINGS OR DISCOUNTS

You will have admission to over 35 attractions on the island of Oahu with the purchase of a Go Oahu card, some of which include Pearl Harbor and the Polynesian Cultural Center. There are passes valid for a single day or for many days that may be purchased.

Thank you for purchasing our travel guide book! We hope you're enjoying it and finding it useful.

We would like to thank you in advance if you decide to go ahead and book your holiday. If you are satisfied with the book, we would appreciate it if you left a review. This allows us to keep providing fantastic travel content and aids other people in making educated travel decisions.

TRAVEL PILOTS